twenties
by bradley cale

isbn-10: 0-692-72045-6
isbn-13: 978-0-692-72045-5

dedicated to my best friend who left this earth far too young. a writer himself, he has always inspired me to write. i love you and i miss you.

thank you to those who have also inspired and supported me along the way: my other best friend in huntington beach, my cousin in newport beach, the teacher in san jose, the comic book writer in los angeles, the graphic designer in los angeles, the real estate broker in manhattan, my creative writing teacher in high school and the jazz singer in austin.

thank you to my poet friends in each of these locations: houston, redondo beach, martinez, mountain house, canada, cocoa beach and stockton. you all know who you are.

thank you to all of my friends i've had the pleasure to connect with on instagram this past year, including you fellow poets and writers. you also know who you are.

and of course - thank you to my family.

oh, and my dog max.

i write in lowercase
because i think
in lowercase.

strawberries hand-
picked, freshly
squeezed irises

stare at me,
these little yellow
grapes on a vine

a straw sun hat
like it's opening day
at del mar racetrack

a belly full of wine
some local,
fruity red blend

and she says
just take me home
and kiss me, this
heat is exhausting

and i can't drive.

empty motel rooms
look like freedom
to a man in jail

the roaches
look like guests,
the flies friends and
invisible lovers lie

on top of dents
in the mattress
the wealthy see filth
the whores see home

and me – i sit here
and i write
about a woman
with eggshell eyes

who sees everything
but what i'd like
her to see.

there's always roadkill
on the 5 freeway
heading to los angeles

the waze app tells me
there's a hazard
on the shoulder

it's a discarded christmas
tree – golden brown
instead of hunter green

abandoned,
no more ornaments
hanging from its branches,
no longer being celebrated

but these passing thoughts
leave my brain
when i reach coalinga

where it always smells
like cow shit.

we just met and
we're at a beach house party
somewhere on the back patio

and she's rolling up a joint
with this pineapple kush and

the bikini she has on
has very little bikini
if you know what i mean

so her beautiful peach tush
is hanging out and it's hard
for me to find the strength

or the self-control
to not steal glances
and rebelution is singing
in the speakers

and she mentions something
about how the waves look
and that she can see a ship
off in the distance

and i swear to you
i've never fallen in love
so quickly before.

the salt ponds
look different up here
at twenty-five
hundred feet

stained glass saliva
dripping
from a foaming mouth

they mean no harm
so i let them
go on with their day

humans in compact cars
slurping milkshakes
navigating

spaghetti junctions
on congested freeways
a cell tower to my left

sends invisible waves
down the mountain
and i can't tell

if the paragliders
are really butterflies

or the other way around.

poems are like days –
you write a shitload
over the years

but in hindsight
only a few are worth
telling your kids about.

scissorhand bushes
lemonade stands
vinyl car stickers

proud parents
of an honor roll student
at fill in the blank
elementary school

adhesive boiling
in a pot on the stove
the 1950s left decades ago

but the tract homes
are still here
and housewives bake
cookie cutter lives
for their husbands, postwar

everyone has discovered
the inkwell filter
is good at

suppressing imperfections
on rear windows
of pickup trucks

driven by old, angry
white men supporting
donald trump

it takes time for color
to transform pleasantville

but let us speed up
the process.

i head over despite her request
and she's sitting at the edge of her bed
cross-legged, no filter, dragging a cigarette

black mascara running down her cheeks
her comforter intertwined with her sheets
her camera on the floor amongst a pile of pictures

she looks at me with these eyes
full of this beautiful twisted agony and says

this is how my mind works
now you've seen it first-hand
and now you can love me, completely

if it all doesn't scare you away...

women have a knack for crawling
into me, effortlessly, pulling
back my layers

and with their gentle hands
pull me from my stubborn mind
reminding me what it's like
to live again

some have tortured me this way
some have loved me this way
some have done both

but all of them, whether it was
a one-night romance
or an entire summer down
in san diego, were worth it

all of them

and i walked away a better man.

honey, i shrunk the kids
was playing in the background
or bill and ted's or back to the future
or a different movie from the 80s

one of them,
and there was a clarinet
being blown in a neighboring garage
by some kid home from college
for the summer

the sliding glass door was cracked
to our backyard
which told me my stepfather
was getting his fix in
before my mother got home

i typed up an away message
on aol instant messenger
that said if anyone wants
to grab a burrito to shoot me a text

i could escape his hidden addiction
i was just worried my little sister
would find out about it.

as artists we will
paint pictures of
surreal places that
corporate employees

will purchase so they
have somewhere
for their mind
to travel

when they get home.

if you want to sense relief
hold your piss in
for a couple hours

if you want heartbreak
go fall in love with the
next handsome
mother fucker
at the bar

and if you want happiness
go get sad, real sad

because that's the only way
you'll know

what happy tastes like.

you take fifty photos
to get the right one

you write fifty poems
and a few come out alright

in my early twenties
after my best friend passed
my doc held out a silver platter
of damn near fifty prescription pills

just try one kid, it's all
just trial and error.

she mentions over text
that she's hesitant to believe
this "pseudo-intellectual-poetic-routine"

isn't just me humoring her onto her back
like some nude literary dance into my bed

where men tend to lead

i scroll up our message thread
to find where she said this
noticing if that's all i wanted

i could have used far fewer words
to convince her that i'm a "gentleman"
rather than an impatient wolf.

i dont want you
to see the world
how i see it, no

i want to share
certain things,
specific things
with you that

i've grown fond of
and hope that you
will notice these
things with me
from now on.

she shows up on my doorstep standing a slim five foot ten with blonde hair up in a ponytail. she has heels in her right hand and a handle of skyy in her left - the devil's advocate herself in a black dress.

"a girl like me shouldn't be walking around campus looking like this at 3 a.m."

i silently agree and let her in as she quickly makes herself at home with bare feet on the coffee table next to two mixed drinks. our couch conversations move to the mattress and sweat into actions as the curtains of my bedroom window sway in the dark. we wake up a quarter past noon on a tuesday, our san diego bodies blended together as one with an old fan oscillating on two young souls just about to fall in love.

i don't love you
anymore

but you're fun
to write about.

by
the
time
we
meet
we've
already
seen the
carefully
marketed
instagram
version of
each other
and become
products of
assumption
walking
down
a

narrow street.

click clack
click clack

the alley cats walk past my window
in high heels at 4 a.m.

they're wrapped in borrowed sweatshirts
covered in cum stains and greek letters
over short, skin-tight dresses

they wake me from my drunken sleep
with their goddamn loud feet

but they walk home content
because they got their fix
and feel that much more beautiful

and the frat boys sleep tight
because they got their fuck
and feel that much more a man

i get up and shut my window.

my grandfather
in a mid-century chair
with a stack of completed
crossword puzzles next to him
takes off his glasses and tells me

you're a young man and then
an old one, all you can do
is try your best

to enjoy the in-between.

you have a ton of followers and your follower to following ratio is on point. i can tell it's well calculated – only a couple people unrequited. they all see you behind your valencia or amaro or earlybird filters. your vintage infused self-portraits. that's what i saw at first and it worked. i fell for the image crafting. it attracted me.

but when the filters started peeling back, when your fake tanning lotion rubbed off on my white sheets, when you removed your makeup every night, when you told me you don't like your teeth, when you'd get a tad insecure in the mornings – that's when i got sucked in.

that's how i always get sucked in.

casual sex is like
wiping your ass
with coffee filters

if you're not careful
it leaves a rash and
in the end you just

want the real thing.

a bearded man writes
poetry alone

at a table
an upright bassline
orders two greyhounds

at the bar
waitresses stack
empty glass cups
up their arms

with grapefruits and
everyone is trying
to find a balance

in here
the hi-hat is spinning
out of control

the bathroom line is long
the atm machine sleeps
and has no money

the jazz band stops
playing
the trumpet player

asks if there
are any big bills
in the jar

and he disappears...

i only come here
for the
carne asada

the salsa
isn't that good

and the owner
is a little rude

at this
dirty taco shop

hotel california
is playing
on a boombox

and
stephen curry
bounces
a basketball

on the spotty
television
in the corner

throughout
life, you will

only visit
certain places
for one thing

and certain
people will
only want one

thing from you.

she drank like a sailor
and swore like a fish

a walking contradiction
everywhere she went.

we're in her bed staring at the ceiling and we have our hands linked up like those chinese finger traps you won at the arcade when you were young. you played all those games like skee ball and whac-a-mole and electronic basketball and you would walk your tickets up to the prize counter and spend an hour deciding what you were going to exchange this paper currency for. maybe you wanted one big prize or a bunch of small prizes. there were foam nunchucks and plastic swords and yo-yos and an assortment of candy. now you're older and this decision making process typically only takes place in the alcohol aisle before a night out. there's rum and gin and whiskey and you end up choosing whatever the girl likes.

we should be at the beach because it's gorgeous outside like it always is in san diego but she only likes going occasionally because she has porcelain skin and prefers overcast weather and doesn't read fashion magazines. she isn't like the other girls down here but that's why i like her. we don't have jobs or any other responsibilities really – only a couple classes a week at grossmont community college. we're in her bed holding hands like chinese finger traps and we're staring at the ceiling and staring into each other's eyes and watching her cat run around the room and after this perfect silence she asks:

"what else is there to do in this world besides write, fuck and model anyways?"

all you can do
is express
yourself

but that
is the least
you must do.

we used to count sheep
now we pop sleep aids
and swipe through human beings
waiting for our dose to kick in

our thumbs act as tools
for romantic hypotheses
sliding pixelated pictures
across smartphone screens

our future husbands and wives
become victims of clumsiness
accidentally swiping them
left instead of right

and they're all out there
in bed alone, just like you
waiting for their dose to kick in.

i'm falling
in love
with
you

from a distance.

i'd never seen hazel
turn that shade of red before
we were stoned and talking about

dr. seuss and i mentioned
that hop on pop was the first book
i ever read

(my grandmother taught me
cuz my pops wasn't around)

and we both said constantinople
or it might've been timbuktu
at the exact same time
and she said

"jinx you owe me a coke!"

"or better yet you owe me some coke"

"actually you don't want to do coke with me"

"because i just ramble and ramble and ramble on"

we held hands and listened to records
and laughed like children
on my bedroom floor.

i can't write without
a thesaurus just like

i don't know what
the fuck to say when

you're in the room.

i met salinger when i was sixteen
hemingway two years later
and bukowski in college

i didn't meet my pops
until right around the time
i could legally drink - he left

when i was two and spent some
time locked up for selling drugs and
probably some other stuff my mother
was happy i wasn't around growing up

so in a way i was raised by a strong woman
and the aforementioned authors
for better or for worse.

we drive by a house with one of those giant circus tents covering it. when i was a kid i really thought there was a circus inside. i'd imagine clowns on stilts, elephants and trapeze artists. but i'm older now. she is sitting in the passenger, feet on the dash.

"disgusting, filthy creatures they are," i say.

"that's your perspective," she responds, "they're actually quite honorable."

"what makes you say that?"

"termites mate for life."

she always throws these little facts out there and i have no clue where she gets them from. after a brief silence, she asks:

"do you think we're meant to mate for life?"

"i think we have the potential to," i respond.

if we give it one
more shot – it has
to be the last time

or else we'll both
become humans
we don't recognize.

she tells me she's an ambivert –
an introvert and an extrovert
simultaneously

like we all have to categorize
ourselves on a shelf
at barnes and noble

self-help
americana
young adult
horror

but i want to live in the margins
of a microsoft word document -
intermingling with the text
or jumping off the page

whenever i please.

if you ask me how to write
i'll say something like -
sit at your desk and
shit it all out

fuck the grammar
fuck the punctuation
fuck the autocorrect and
fuck the three-prong thesis

i can punch an algorithm
into a robot for all that

but that's not truth
and that's not you
and that's not who you are

when you ain't got anyone
tellin' you what to do
so just shit it out

and worry about
the mess you've made later.

who's to say
true love isn't
just sucking

each other's
blood and
symbiotically
spooning in
dirty sheets

while watching
seinfeld reruns
on a monday
afternoon?

so you try to become someone new
and someone remembers
how you used to be

and they say that's who you are
and that's who you should be
and you're not like this new person
they've been seein' lately

"you're a hypocrite"

well that's the definition of someone
holding back your growth
because they're scared
or they're grasping at comfort

but imagine if that prevented you
from shedding old skin
or becoming a better person

your old tweets don't define you
your old mistakes don't define you
just go with how you feel right now

because that's who you are.

love tends
to work out
better when

you don't
need it.

they're all plugged in. they're all on adderall and they're all plugged in - into laptops, into smartphones, into this third dimension that's been created without anyone really noticing. it's the love library at san diego state but it could be any library on any college campus really. it's 2007 and i look down at my hands and my fingers and begin to think they're now just limbs used to relay information in this social media network of the next generation. to text and tweet and create alternative personalities. i notice four students sitting around a table ignoring one another, spinning in wheels, mouths dry, pupils dilated from the prescribed amphetamines that will help them crunch out their take-home exams in limited time - even if it takes all night. i hit a solo desk nearby and reach into my pocket for this magnificent new orange pill – to join them.

ask me questions
no question
marks

no marks at all
no punctuation
just whatever

rolls off your tongue.

artifacts found
in makeshift rafters
of mom's attic

include rookie cards
of baseball players
that didn't perform

well enough
to be worth anything
to collectors

hoarders of card stock
memories, slanted
smiles of hope

thousands
of talented athletes
never made it
in the big league

thousands
didn't realize
their dreams

these cards of failure
are worth more to me.

i sat in my car
for an hour
outside my gym

waiting

for the rain to
subside so i
could run in

while

she was at home
watching old
sitcoms

waiting

for them to end
and we texted
each other
while we
waited

for us to begin.

you try to wait
until you can
give someone
your best self

but

sometimes
someone can
turn you into
your best self.

i'm at my desk and everyone around me are tapping pencils or clicking french manicured nails on cell phone keys. my teacher mumbles through a lecture and the students scribble notes they'll never look at. the clock hand hits 12:15 p.m. and everyone seems to disappear.

next class isn't until 6:10, so i head over to golden gate park. two tan kids are lying on the lawn drinking pabst blue ribbon out of cans. the boy smokes a cigarette and the girl reads a novel she picked up at a used bookstore in the haight. the sun reflects off their slender bodies like it does each individual blade of grass, reflecting back into the san francisco sky.

i hop on a bus and head downtown for some food. i get off on powell and buy a bracelet from a nice old man sitting at a small tent on market. there's a bum on the sidewalk holding a cardboard sign that reads "$1 for good carma" - just like that. i drop two.

i run into a businessman turning a corner up the street and he looks at me with an angry face, collar tight and forehead glistening with perspiration. probably running late to some fancy appointment, or maybe to meet a mistress at the dive motel off mission. another one drives up in a sports car, arguing with himself at a red light with an electronic stick attached to his ear. a trolley inhabited by tourists clicks by and someone snaps a photo of me. oh well.

now i'm sitting in the middle of union square with a sandwich and a carbonated water and all these humans are walking around me with swift footsteps and designer purses. i start to think about the kids in golden gate park and the old man at the tent and the bum and his cardboard sign. the sun hits my face and i take a bite and a drop of mayonnaise drips down my cheek.

everyone seems to disappear, again.

we’re all still kids
searching for

the lunch table
we want to sit at.

i say i want to make love
to this song
in an empty apartment

she says she is
an empty apartment

no sheets
no comforter
not even a box spring

there's a spider hanging
from the ceiling and
i think i saw a
roach in the
bathroom

but we got jazz
and we got blues

and she has a place
to rest her head
tonight.

it was valentine's day and
i wore a pinstriped pink collared shirt
with grey slacks and shiny shoes

she wore french manicured nails
with blonde curls and a red dress
that was painted on her body

i was dressed to impress
and she was dressed to kill
the night would be perfect

but mapquest isn't always honest
and she started stressing out
when i couldn't find the restaurant

and when i did
we had lost our reservations
and in her mind it was all my fault

"let's go to a diner"

but she just shook her head
and lit a cigarette and said
we were way too overdressed

she didn't smoke too often
but when she did
i knew the night was over.

if you swallow a spider
even a venomous one
your stomach acid
will take care of it
before it has
the chance
to strike
your

internal organs
the reality of this is
that you were made to
survive more than you think.

the palm trees in santa monica
fell apart last weekend
due to a storm

that no one in los angeles
knows how to drive in

i saw people fall apart
on sunset boulevard
the night before

but a homeless man with a guitar
while pissing on a hollywood star

said that's just rock 'n' roll.

an 8.9 earthquake tsunami
just hit japan and gosh

i really hope it doesn't
make it out here because

i'm sitting in an office chair
drunk and in my underwear.

she would sit in a plush leather loveseat
at bloomingdale's and sketch
all the housewives shopping

for two thousand dollar handbags
made overseas and she'd pretend
to shop a little between that
and people watching

because if they thought
you were a customer
you'd get free martinis

and she'd devour the olive and say
that's all we're doing anyways,
just pretending.

fall in love with
someone who
enjoys the
simple
things
in life

and
they will
enjoy the
simple things
inside of you.

i can feel her in the form
of book antiqua words
on perfectly cropped
white walls

i can feel her electric heart
beating beneath
my thumbprint

on my instagram feed

it's like walking the streets
of the forbidden city
on google maps

i can't climb the stone steps
to her warm soul
i can't drop a little pin
on certain coordinates
of her mind

i can't touch her
i can't taste her
i can't experience her

how i want to.

i don't have metaphors
or similes or any
other poetic
techniques

to cover up the fact
that i'm being a wimp
for i can't man up
sober and

tell you anything
that makes me
vulnerable

and you're a better writer
than me, anyways

but when a can of paint
spills, it
spills

and you can perceive it
as street art
or graffiti
or a colorful mess
or however you want

i just hope you won't
apply an asterisk
to a mural

i painted for you.

we won’t start living
until the receptors
on our tongues

learn to enjoy
all the madness
that rolls off them.

i met a man at a bar
straight out of a spaghetti western
and he told me that life looks better
in black and white

he put some money in the jukebox
and said: "kid, pick some tunes -
just nunna that shit i hear
on the radio these days,
those songs barely
last a week"

i threw on
some cash
some clapton
some b.b. king

and a girl asked me (later in the night)
what color hair i prefer
and i responded:

"it's all the goddamn same
when ya gotta face that
transcends decades
like yours."

so many thoughts are deleted
by that measly plastic
backspace button

rip that fucker off and
let them spill from
your fingers

like this poem.

i've met all my moods. we're on a first name basis and i know what they drink right when they walk through the door. eye contact and a double shot of scotch coming right up. or a whiskey water with a slice of lemon. it just depends. one is sitting across from me as we speak, ashing on my nightstand between drags. he's wearing a black top hat and telling me every little thing i did wrong today. but his visits are typically short and when the morning comes i have a brand new visitor who is much more pleasant. he hangs his coat on the appropriate rack and doesn't leave cigarette butts in my toilet. i've met all my moods - they come often and leave quickly but i don't fight them, just try to welcome their company and allow life to run its sporadic course.

if i can’t have
all of you

i don’t want
any of you.

we're sitting at the denny's off the 8 freeway just passed san diego state. she's in a white t-shirt with 'the cure' written across her chest, some jeans that are ripped at the knees and rainbow sandals. her hair is damp in a braid down her shoulder. i order a black coffee, she has an orange juice. her legs are crossed up on the booth and she's texting someone (a friend) so i pick up the newspaper, glance over a few headlines and put it down again.

i look at the table to my right - a couple with their kids. one around 3 or 4 sitting in a booster seat, the other around 1 in a high chair in the walkway. the waitresses have to walk around him with dishes balanced up their arms. little guy is creating quite the traffic jam. he's throwing food on the floor and going in and out of cries. i'm annoyed. she won't look up from her phone, so i just start talking. sometimes spitting it out is the best approach.

"i don't think i meant what i said last night."

why explain how you feel
when you can create
a pattern of emojis
with hidden
messages

that they will spend hours
trying to decipher if
they really care.

she heads over after midnight
and he’s on the back patio
in a wicker chair
sucking on a joint full of bone marrow

his handsome words rolling off his tongue
and crawling up her spine
as they share clever conversation
before he grabs her leg and mentions

“let’s remove our hearts from this
to avoid any messiness”

like she’s a surgeon and it’s an easy game
of operation for adult organisms
to tweeze out emotions
with shivering hands

just to satisfy one particular organ
of his chiseled body.

you’re only flustered
because you can’t fit me
in a tiny little box

like you put everyone else in
so delicately on your bookshelf
wrapped in a bow.

i could watch her play piano for hours as she flips through music sheets complaining about the missing pages. she says something like “i’m a little rusty” but i don’t notice and she plays anyways, right through her frustration. she attempts to be perfect in a realm that demands perfection. i say imperfections make it all worth a damn. she tells me she hasn’t missed a note during a recital her entire 21 years. except for once. she cried the entire way home.

i can’t help but think i missed a note last week, making her a little distant. now i wish i could rip the goddamn sheet out and we could play something different, after tonight.

maybe they live
in a shade of yellow

and we live
in a shade of blue

maybe our love
is dark and cynical

maybe their optimism
isn't true.

we rolled over
and let out two big sighs
and she rolled back
and placed her hand on my chest

as i stared at the ceiling
collecting my thoughts
and she said

"please don't write
a dirty little poem
about me"

so i didn't.

the bittersweet taste of coronas
and salted limes on lips
the electronic music
our electronic hearts

synchronized, we dance frozen
in time - flashing neon lights
illuminate the room

like her smile
her silhouette in strobe
silver dress, bites her lip
blue eyes, blonde hair

cinnamon skin, another sip
grabs my hand and puts it on her hip
van buuren, benassi

the music controls our bodies
go outside, a fountain on the patio
lights hanging from the lattice

a cigarette over conversation
or conversation over a cigarette
she drops it, we laugh, i light it again

go inside, a shot, another exchange
smiles, a couple witty lines
back and forth

we leave the bar
stumble down the steps
wave a cab and music keeps playing

strangers keep dancing into the night...

i was piss drunk dead
at the bar when we met

but she dragged me
out onto the dance floor
put her hand on my chest
and said

let the bass
inside your heart
and it won't stop beating.

right click, view, large icons
of everything and
everyone in
your life

right click, sort by, item type
only those that
are holding
you back

left click, highlight
all said folders and
all their contents
drag and drop
in recycle bin

right click, empty

are you sure you want
to permanently delete
these 24 items?

fuck yes!

right click, refresh.

i have too much art on my walls
and not enough empty wall space

while you have too many walls
around your empty heart.

it's been a long night and everyone is still dancing. look at them all – manikins in masquerade masks moving their limbs under chauffeured ceilings. sweating to death in two thousand dollar chanel dresses and bow tied men with red clammy faces spilling drinks on ebony floors. some people look better in the window.

"let's get out of here before the lights turn on and the truth comes out."

she grabs her purse as i leave the tip and we're right where we want each other – walking back to my apartment holding hands within the darkness and pretending we're something much more than what our sober minds will come to grips with tomorrow morning, when the masks come off.

don’t you love it
when you feel yourself
becoming yourself again

tell me you love it
when a smile breaks
that you can’t resist

it just breaks –
and the sun swarms in
and fills your chest

with a warmth
you haven’t felt for years

don’t you love it
when your lips break
and not your heart

and nothing shatters
but waves
against the shore.

she sits across from me silently stirring her starbucks made light with a dash of cinnamon and a double shot of espresso - just how she likes it. her bangs rest softly on her forehead with her hair straightened just past her shoulders and her legs crossed at the knees causing her dress to hike up and reveal two tan slender thighs - just how i like it. she blows around the rim of her paper cup and complains they always make it too hot but takes a sip anyways, leaving a lipstick stain on the perimeter.

"so, how are you?"

"i'm doing well."

"and the writing?"

"coming along."

"i'm glad."

she forces a smile and shrugs her shoulders and then it hit me and i got my closure for when passionately fucking in bedrooms turns into casual conversation in coffee shops, you know the love is gone.

i ask her what she does
with her friday nights
and she tells me

she spends hours clicking
around on facebook until
she feels really really small

and then smokes a pack
of cigarettes on her patio
wrapped in her favorite
american apparel sweatshirt

that reminds her of him.

we’re good people
and i still love you

i just think we are
two different chemicals
that are destructive

when combined.

20s were
killing time
chasing girls
chasing highs
collecting debt
getting out of it
breaking hearts
getting mine broken
diving to the bottom
swimming to the top
treading water like a dog
clawing at the rocky shore
putting all the puzzle pieces

b a c k t o g e t h e r

saying fuck it
taking a deep breath and
jumping right back in the water.

the bartender leans in
because house music is blaring
from the speakers

and we can barely get a word in
to each other and he says

you don't see too many
like her around here

she's a rose in a whiskey glass,
a beautiful girl but she burns
like hell going down.

society will
think you’re
going crazy

when you’re
going sane.

cheap love is all
i'm interested in
at the moment

a $4.99 bottle of fish eye
on the conveyor belt
next to a pack of gum
and trojan condoms

any wine with
a twist-off cap
to be honest

under her breath
the checker says
"looks like a fun night"

maybe next week
it'll be different
or next year

maybe then
i'll be ready
for what you want.

i know she's
not mine
all the time

but she's
mine tonight

let it roll.

i might get evicted on the 5th
for not paying rent

and my checking account
is overdrawn $124.92

and i owe $56.16
to san diego gas and electric
and another $41.95 for cable

but there is a six pack
of grolsch in my fridge

a fresh pack of marlboro lights
on my nightstand

and a quarter bottle of whiskey
staring at me on my desk.

you cannot
fix anyone

only briefly
distract them
from what
makes them

broken.

it just happens and you're staring at the lines of your pale hands searching for answers and picking at scabs. it just happens and you're sitting cross-legged in showers slapping plexiglass walls. it just happens and you wake up to a phone call that will forever change your life. it just happens and you're bouncing a ball in your backyard for hours until your grandmother offers a cigarette to ease your mind.

you don't believe it until you turn the corner and see the red lights of an ambulance pulling away. you don't believe it until you're at michaels buying candles for his vigil at st. augustines. you don't believe it until you see him lying in an open casket with rosary beads resting within his motionless fingers.

i wanted to shake him until he woke up.

you don't believe it until you're searching the internet for what a pallbearer wears to a funeral. until you see a white hearse pull in front of a catholic church. the driver gets out and tells us "this one is heavy, it's made of oak."

you don't believe it until you're staring at a box covered in cloth surrounded by hundreds of mourning people. until the priest reads an irish blessing and everyone is forced to say goodbye. until you see his family release balloons of his favorite color into the afternoon sky. an incredibly tragic ending to a storybook life.

"a spark produces its brightest glow just before it dies."

how many times do you
rearrange your room
before you realize

it's you?

invisible people walk along crosswalks. gigantic trains roar by and disappear into the night. everyone around you are projections of your thoughts in response to premeditated expectations of the present situation. a rushed encounter at the supermarket or a lunch meeting with a potential lover. chameleons survive in the wild by adapting to their environment. she decides which fork to use as the waiter brings your food. red lipstick and a faded black apron are colors perceived by sight and your other four senses pick and choose what to notice. the cook spins a salad in the back and you can't help but overhear conversations from neighboring tables as invisible people walk along crosswalks outside with their hands covered in grease and wet paint splattered all over their shoes.

i've walked into
every single boutique
downtown, twice now
looking for something
i'll never find

i ran into my late best friend
in his favorite jersey
at the cafe on the corner

and now i'm writing poems
in my sleep

will someone please
just wake me up.

flowers still bloom
in graveyards
of the american dream

occasionally, but
the middle class
needs water

before decaying
completely, because
hairspray only works

on dead roses
and aerosol cans
are hazardous waste

and you can also
tie the stems together
and hang them
upside down

and we're talking about
hard working people here
who can't eat without
food stamps, struggling

to find employment
so they sell drugs
or their bodies
to pay rent, yeah

flowers may still bloom
in the ashes
of the top one percent

but we need a little help
not in the form
of a handout

just some more balance.

people - they love to talk. they sit behind desks with fluorescent smiles and neon highlighters and shuffle papers prepared by who knows who. i watch them on mute in high-definition as their lips flap like ventriloquist dolls behind pressed suits and wooden expressions. and we'll bite on every single word they say because our generation has come to believe every goddamn thing we see on television and our twitter feeds. just remember that these so-called experts, anchors, critics, analysts, politicians, professionals, authority figures, et cetera...

all did dirty things to themselves in the shower this very morning –
i promise you.

it’s okay to get close
to self-destruction
sometimes

nothing motivates
idle hands more
than a ticking bomb.

i slept great
the train didn't drive by last night

no horn
no tracks
no one

getting anywhere anytime soon
the precious cargo can wait
until morning

it usually wakes me up
every goddamn time it roars by

at 1 a.m.
and again at 4

but you didn't call
and i slept great

what's going on?

fireworks from far away burn the sky black with color - to the south over dana point, to the east over newport harbor, to the north over huntington and above catalina island in the middle of the pacific. they burn the sky black and fade away like ex-lovers with new fiancés.

life is temporary.

a girl behind me laughs and says the smiley face makes her day. the declaration tried to give us independence – a breakup letter is liberation with a broken heart. ambivalence bleeds red, white and blue tonight as i watch the metallic willows and the neon palm trees and the roman candles explode from this sandy blanket and they all combust at their highest points.

i just can't see where they land.

you won't get independence
from a constitution

the shackles come off
when you don't rely
on anyone for anything -

that's when you're free.

i'm prepared to meet you
like the man unloading
fire extinguishers
lined up in a row

or the woman
carrying an umbrella
with no chance of rain

in the parking garage
of the office building
on my way to work.

2 or 3 weeks before he passed i tried the pill that took my best friend. the pill form of heroin - a pill called opana. he took it for an injured foot and mixed it with too many shots of whiskey. i took it purely recreationally and not only tried it but a different friend cut it up and i sniffed it up my nose through a twenty-dollar bill - mimicking what i always saw in the movies. this different friend got it from some doctor who had a trigger hand for writing prescriptions. doctors and lawyers have the worst handwriting.

2 or 3 weeks before he passed i tried the drug that took my best friend. i was at a ranch house in livermore, it was 3 a.m. and there was a beautiful girl waiting for me in the spare bedroom. i sat in the backyard staring off into the distance, numb as fuck, no anxious thoughts, not a single worry on my mind. i smiled, a big smile and just sat there in this wicker chair thinking about jack shit but how fucking great i felt. i'd never experienced a sense of peace like that before. but it was fake peace – you couldn't touch it.

eventually i got the strength to control my legs, walked into the room and the beautiful girl pleasured me, pleasured me real good, but i couldn't get my dick up. the next morning i told myself i'd never take that drug again.

i try to count sheep
but all i see

are pretty girls
driving expensive cars

and buildings
made of legos on

my morning commute.

bukowski bet horses,
pete rose bet baseball
when he shouldn't have

and i put all my change
i found under
my sofa cushions on red

told the dealer
to spin the cylinder
because just like the
aforementioned

i'm a ramblin' / gamblin'
piss drunk man tonight

and russian roulette
is all i have left.

drunken motorcycles laughter
garbage sweepers street trucks
sirens the mailman in high heels
still buzzed from the night before

and a homeless woman rambling
out loud to herself while i am
sprawled across the carpet
in my apartment doing

the same damn thing in my head.

these men
in nascar jackets
with packed tobacco lips

spend their dollars
on old country songs
from the digital jukebox

and california lottery tickets
hoping to win, hoping
they won't have to

drown their dreams
in bottles of beer every week
for the rest of their lives

hoping that a combination
of six random numbers
will grant them
their freedom

in this dive bar of a universe.

there's a difference
between traveling
the world with
someone

and going on
vacation with them
zipped in their suitcase.

she tells me she doesn't need me to say anything. she just needs me to be the dial tone she used to talk to as a child while her parents were fighting in the other room. she doesn't need any reactions, she just needs me to be the popcorn ceiling she stares at every night as the fan spins in her mind and her tiny feet walk the eggshell walls of her skull.

"this ambien makes counting sheep more fun / they change colors like the horse in the wizard of oz."

i can taste her breath over the phone, i can feel it on my neck, i can hear her heartbeat popping in her microwave chest. i'm somewhere over here in my studio apartment and she's somewhere over there in a suburban town and somewhere between us is a tower made out of aluminum foil feeding her digital voice to my hollow ear.

"i wish we could use walkie talkies but you're too far away / i hear these cellular devices cook us from the outside in."

i watch my fish swim around the bowl on my kitchen counter and wonder how the invisible radio waves are affecting him. i ask her if she likes bettas and she tells me she wishes she had a long flowing tail and metallic skin. i tell her she can have anything she dreams of, even a castle at the bottom of the ocean and she responds that she's only had nightmares lately and she's feeling tired and she doesn't want to be rude because i've been so patient but she really needs to get some rest.

dear stranger –
that ain't you, no
that ain't you

those are just symptoms
of your situation and
the good news is

it's a helluva lot
easier to change
your situation

than it is to change you.

you start sharing
glances
chopsticks
text messages
forks, comforters
saliva, sweat, stories
netflix account passwords

you drag and drop
your entire life into
their spotify playlist but

how easily it goes from that
to regret, memories, old
photographs and empty
bottles of wine on
your balcony.

she's at her vanity, hair up in a towel,
struggling with her cat eye
as she reapplies makeup
between half-naked shots of bacardi, no chase

her friends are somewhere
she was supposed to be hours ago
but this is her favorite part of the night

getting ready by herself to oldies
while texting thirsty fuckboys with alibis
when they ask her what time she'll show up

she knows beauty isn't rushed

and she's reminded of a poem by ezra pound
that took him a year-and-a-half to cut down
30 lines to 3

and most of it's in the title
and most of it's in the eyes
and most of the time we are all

just rough drafts that need plenty of editing.

maybe we don’t
grow tired of lovers

maybe we grow
tired of the routine

we build with them.

all kinds of birds
gather on power lines
after their morning coffee

and shoot the shit
under water cooler clouds
planning vacations down south

while neighborhood boys
toss sneakers into the
turquoise sky

where they tangle up
like headphones
and a man

in a classic chevelle roars by
burning gas from the
fountain of youth

a woman around twenty-five
in a floral pattern dress
has all of this in view

from a cafe nearby
where saxophone sounds
vibrate from the speakers inside

they've conquered the day -
the birds, the woman,
the man, the boys

queens and kings of the sun
while everyone else
is slaving away.

the poets
the artists
the musicians

they struggle out loud
while the boring
businessmen

keep it inside
to collect currency
like a stirring wildfire

that wants to spread out.

let's tell 'em to
sit in a car
sit in a desk
sit in a cube

let's pass out prescription pills
in ice cream trucks
and tell them they can't smoke weed
even if they want to

i'll take an adderall / lexapro swirl
with an ambien on top
please mr. ice cream man!

let's pay 'em bi-weekly for some
good old positive reinforcement

(a rat will continuously press a lever
for the rest of their life if you
give them food in intervals)

they say it's hard work
but they pay me for my time
and not my production

let's tell 'em to sit in a cube
until they're lying in a coffin

that's fine doc, i just have one request –
please let me bring my phone
so if i get claustrophobic
six feet under

i can order my medicine via a text.

fuck all the
mushy-love-poem-
romantic-bullshit...

i just want someone
to get drunk at
disneyland with.

“there’s something on your mind tonight.”

“i don’t really know how to put it into words...

...it’s just, life seems like it never stops. i don’t know if it’s this city, if this is how it’s supposed to be, or if it’s just me. i honestly get anxious when i sit down. i always have to be doing something – filling silence, writing something in my day planner, texting someone while i’m in the elevator, fidgeting with the forks at the dinner table. i always need an action or a plan or i lose a sense of control and it freaks me out.”

“that isn’t necessarily a bad thing.”

“but what do we do when we run out of plans, when there’s nothing left?”

“that’s just it, we won’t. we’ll keep making them, keep moving, like every other organism does until they die.”

you tip your hat
to the man at the bar
you tell him
there's plenty of room
for a dark horse

you tell him
you might not
light up the room
but you sure as hell
know how to dim it
the perfect shade of blue

that's what you'll tell him
when he asks why you
don't smile with your
pretty scarlet lips

when you drink alone.

we'd still be together
if you stared at me

the way you stare at
your smartphone screen.

when did we become
these dispensable beings
engaging in snippet relationships
swiping strangers on rectangular screens

twirling them in and out of our lives
like some casual 21st century
ballroom dance routine

on sticky laminate tiles
in high heels and wingtip oxfords
every week we foxtrot with new partners

recycling paper-thin words
and aluminum feelings
just to talk them back to our apartments

twenty-something hipsters
in ikea-filled lofts living
synapse to synapse
futon to futon
high to high

treating one another
like disposable cameras
and capturing moments
with no intent of developing the film

anytime soon.

i saw this beautiful man in the financial district
wearing an expensive suit, so expensive
i knew he was ugly between the seams

turned the corner and saw this homeless man
with these rotten teeth and this saggy skin
and all these wrinkles

and he had this torn up flannel on
and velcro shoes and he was so damn ugly

i knew he was beautiful.

we’ve gotta
let humans
be human

even if it’s
human to
crave control.

dating seems like a multiple choice
test nowadays that involves
destructive reasoning

the fuckboys of tinder
the attention whores of instagram
the killjoys of match.com

take your pick

with so many options at our fingertips
it's no surprise the divorce rate
is on a steady ascent

but are we all genuinely like this
or have these cell phone apps
our generation has eagerly created
designed to bring us together -

have they really just torn us apart?

i was driving to work one day and a man in a tailored suit and the smell of expensive musk appeared in my passenger with a twelve gauge on his lap. or maybe he was just riding shotgun. regardless, he grabbed my shoulder firmly and with his chin cocked and a pair of passionate eyes looked at me and said:

"kid, you live your life worrying about those people in their cars on the other side of the freeway and what they think - you'll spend it on your knees with your hands behind your back and society's gun down your throat. remember, they're moving in the opposite direction."

he slapped my cheek and told me to grip the steering wheel like a man.

"now kid, you throw some dark shades on with a little attitude on your shoulder and disregard that rearview and keep your eyes between the two lines there and gas it – that's when you'll drive life to perfect success."

and just like that, he was gone.

as the products
peeled off her body
like unnecessary skin

the ray-ban sunglasses
the michael kors purse
the crest whitestrip teeth
the 7 for all mankind jeans
the christian louboutin shoes
the victoria secret bra and panties

she stood there naked and gorgeous
not because she was nude
but because she was no longer

an advertisement.

these people with their so-called perfect lives
walking out of corner restaurants
after 5 p.m. cocktails, suits and all

their laughter filling brick-lined alleyways
echoing into city windows
just as the sun goes down

i'll admire them
and ponder for a moment
how the hell they have it all figured out

but then i'll head home
and situate myself with you
between your legs wrapped around my hips
on the floor of my studio apartment

a record spinning
our minds drunk off the gallon of wine
that we typically forget to put a cork in

there's always a little that seems to go to waste

they don't have this -
the comfort of this floor
the comfort of your embrace

they don't have you
and that's all i need.

he usually falls for the
damsel in distress but

hasn’t quite figured out
what it takes to be the

knight in shining armor.

you sit at your desk long enough and everything begins to come alive. scissors hop out of pencil cups and walk around on steel legs. staplers chatter their teeth spitting up metal limbs. binder clips turn into spiders and bite at your arms. paper clips connect to one another like those red plastic monkeys and swing around from thumbtack to thumbtack pushed into your cubical walls that display old photographs and the interoffice phone list. these tools of capitalism become your friends and you head down the hall to the supply room for containers to organize them in. you catch yourself talking to them sporadically and they never respond and the rest of the time you're not working you stare at your mouse pad with an exotic locale on it with palm trees and a beach and bright blue waves and every morning after the fourth time you press snooze you wake up and think about bringing your swim trunks to work and jumping headfirst into the tropical paradise you fixate on all day.

she leans in and tells me
the last time
she heard this song
she was on ecstasy
and then she kisses me

like somehow certain music
can teleport your mind
to all of the times
you've felt free

or maybe that's just the mdma -
regardless, it was the best kiss

i've had in a while.

stop trying to
convince people

to understand
your weirdness

just find some
who already do

who are fucking
weird, like you.

a white pill sits in the palm of my friend's hand. "triple stacked," he says. he got it from some kid he met at a party last weekend in long beach. he hands me a bottle of water and tells me to make him a promise.

"promise me you understand that whatever you feel tonight will never be replicated for the rest of your life. when you get your dream job after college, when you meet your wife, when you get married, when you have your firstborn child. nothing will make you feel as good as this white pill."

i take it and we head to the electric daisy carnival at memorial coliseum in los angeles two weeks after michael jackson died. we pass by the usc marching band on the way in as the ecstasy hits and the snare drums rattle in my head like maracas and we walk down the concrete steps watching the gigantic ferris wheel spin.

kaskade opens his set with skream's in for the kill remix and all these pretty girls are on stilts wearing neon colors and barely nothing else and the bass drops and lights flash as two lesbians kiss and ask me if i want my shoulders rubbed. david guetta comes on and you have full access to the entire place so i walk up to the very top to watch the fireworks explode and for the first time in my life i feel like the world is truly mine.

i've never seen one hundred thousand people move their limbs in the exact same motion at the exact same time before. i've never felt my spine vibrate, i've never tasted bliss quite like this and i've never felt so free and i wake up the next morning in an afterglow hoping my friend was dead wrong about what he said.

we’ll jump through the hoops of capitalism
we’ll pay interest on the loans for school

we’ll earn that fancy piece of bond paper
that acts as a glorified marketing tool

we used to gather wild plants
we used to hunt for wild animals

but now we’ll spend hours in cages
collecting the necessary wages

to survive in this world.

a woman with steel ovaries
walks into a bar
buys herself a drink
and lights her own cigarette

while men with shriveled balls
are turned off by her success

i sense tension between the sexes
a confused culture
of adult adolescents

dudes swiping tinder to fuck
ladies giving sex to get love
sending nudies on snapchat
and watching them disappear

we've got boys raised with
mad men ideas of gender roles
getting sucked off by secretaries

in corner offices
that women now occupy
floor to ceiling windows
instead of invisible glass ceilings

resulting in shattered egos
and testosterone fueled
insecurities

no one said this would be easy
just necessary.

you wanted to
be friends but

cold turkey

was the only
way to quit you.

it's cold in my apartment
for winter is here, suddenly
and i haven't had someone out
from the gas and electric company
to light my pilot

i suppose i could do it myself...
anyways, it's a little warmer

when you're around
when our naked body heat
starts a little flame in my bed
after we collect resin
from the pine trees

in the wilderness of our hearts
and use it for tinder
and you whisper

this is the only way to survive
a snowstorm.

there's no place for miniature hawaiian umbrellas anywhere. only small talk on toothpicks over pineapple frozen yogurt topped with cheesecake and fresh strawberries. a spontaneous lunch with an old friend who makes ten dollar sunglasses from a mall kiosk look like five hundred bucks. we notice a girl (around 21) sitting next to us, lathering her lips with unflavored chapstick ignoring the kids she nannies during summer and disregarding what really matters but we understand as i read my thoughts about hollywood stored in my blackberry. i point out the window at an elderly couple struggling to unload books next door and she looks and wonders what is really under the covers. she wants to grab one to read before bed but the unknown is also satisfying. we get up to leave and find ourselves with a decision to abide by certain rules where there is no place for miniature hawaiian umbrellas anywhere so we compromise on napkins and a hug goodbye and head back to work.

she pours her heart out
to a homeless man

outside an abandoned
roman catholic church

on a buzzed walk home
from the bars one night

he offers a cigarette
the last one he has left

and with stained glass eyes
and whiskey on her breath

she tells this urban priest
all of her sins

because it's a helluva lot
easier to ask strangers

for forgiveness.

you're not at liberty to say
i hate you

if you've never said
i love you.

i was at baja fresh for lunch enjoying a burrito and running a little late back to the office and i asked an older gentleman seated across if i could steal his time and he said:

“absolutely not young man – i don’t know you and i don’t just give the one thing that matters most to me to strangers, especially ones with dark eyes like you.”

he cleaned up his lunch in a disgruntled hurry and got up and threw everything in the garbage by the door including the tray.

next time i’ll remember to point at my wrist.

how come
we despise
the nine-to-five

but when
we leave it
we are scared
of ourselves

are we little mice
trained for routine
trained for battle
trained for heartbreak
trained to purchase

everything just to
throw it all away?

if that's what we are
pour me another drink
pour me your heart
into my glass

and let me set it free.

yesterday over cocktails
a friend mentioned
the world is a different place

that monogamy doesn't exist
when we're all so interconnected
and moving at such a fast pace

she wants a weekday lover
a weekend lover
a lover for every state of mind

this got me wondering
where i fit in this world
with a heart that burns like mine.

were our flaws
really flaws

or were they
just symptoms

of two souls
that grew sick

of each other?

i don't take compliments well
i often order my drinks well
i've bounced more
quarters into
shot glasses

than wishing wells
because superstitions
aren't money well spent

and well, that's about it for today.

oxycontin and alcohol
two deadly drugs dancing
to your destruction

as angels in white lab coats
and teal scrubs struggle
to keep you alive

new habits develop
so easily and we all know
they sure as hell die hard

coffee to wake up
melatonin to fall asleep

rockstar and whiskey
adderall and ambien
cocaine and heroin

it's all the same
just different degrees

an ethics book told me
in community college
everything's okay
in moderation

even honesty
even excess
even ignorance

is fucking bliss, sometimes
until the consequences
say hello and goodbye
simultaneously.

it's a helluva lot harder
to find someone when
you're a little different

but once you do
you'll sure as hell find
it's a different kind of love

worth the persistence.

sometimes when i want to lose control
i exit spotify and open a brand new
internet browser tab

i type in pandora's address
and rip my headphones out
speakers full blast

it turns my perfectly organized playlists
into a randomized song generator
based on an algorithm
i'll never understand

sometimes songs sound so much better
when they come on the radio themselves

not picked
not forced
not chosen

just fate

and sometimes it's so much better
when humans enter
our lives this way.

i love being written off by people -
it's like a free refill of black ink

that i'll use to write them
a thank you letter when i arrive

at where they thought i wouldn't go.

we can all stare across
our local dance clubs
with hate on our faces
in overpriced
bottle service booths

and gossip about
who went home with who,
who's ugly, who's broke,
who has a venereal disease

as some kind of sick way
to satisfy our fragile egos

or

we can join tables
have positive conversations
lick one another's wounds

and realize we're all in this
goddamn struggle together.

it's a mess like this poem. wordsjumbledtogether, commas; and punctuation! outof place like my hair after waking up on couches: puzzle pieces scattered on the kitchentable. my room, usually! spotless has: laundry and hangers and blankets and bottle caps and bills, pictures of you strewn about everywhere on the floor. my guitar, stringless and un-tuned. i can't play/i can't write/mythoughtsmywordsmyactions NONSENSE! i sit at work stacks of paper post-its pencils my pants my shirt my life wrinkled and a goddamn iron is nowhere to be found...

i want to get drunk
enough to forget you

but not too drunk
that i'll miss you.

my grandfather told me
over the phone yesterday

"your grandmother tricked me
into marrying her – she said
her pops was in the oil
industry but little
did i know

that meant he worked
at the gas station
on the corner"

we both laughed
and hung up shortly after
and then i made a mental note

that no matter how old i get
i can't forget to have
a sense of humor.

there's a spider
who lives in my bathroom
and i think she likes the cure

she once spun a web
to friday i'm in love
i watched her

in the past
(when i was a young man)
i might've squashed her

because we're taught
to destroy things that we fear

but now if she needs
a little blood at night

she can feel free and suck mine
or if she wants to dance alone
while i'm at my typewriter

she's more than welcome.

"we won't step foot
around here again
until it's gentrified

until capitalism
has run its course
and the strong survive"

an old man to his kids
rushing them home
to suburbia

in a range rover
back to nice schools
and tree-lined streets

where the children
argue over iphones
and whose dad owns
a high-definition television

back to a town
with no art and culture
and no life and no soul

but they're safe
and they can ignore
a systematic structure

that tends to test
those who are born
in environments
with far less resources

much, much more.

look at them all - sucking on cigarettes, standing in line for subway trains while scanning over the morning news. headlines stir worry and they all start panting and grinding their teeth anxiously. insecure animals they are.

look at them - getting their hourly fix of caffeine from caramel macchiatos and constantly checking watches, running late like always.

humans wrapped up in long trench coats holding briefcases or wearing white blouses tucked into black pencil skirts and wool coats religiously reading text messages on blackberrys and talking to themselves with electronic sticks in their ears. doors open and they rush in, flocks of them. the train starts and stops. starts and stops. metropolis without the flying cars.

doors open again and they disperse to their nine-to-fives and it all begins: selling stocks, making copies, tapping pencils, shooting the shit over the water cooler. office buildings act as pens and the entire world's a farm.

now it's happy hour and everyone is well, happy. sitting at bars escaping reality and coping with stress using mechanisms they can't seem to shed. cougars with silicone tits and orange skin hitting on twenty-one-year-old boys in tech and married attorneys secretly meeting virgins after work for cocktails.

when you are young you want to be older but when you're old you crave to be young again.

hopped up and feeling dirty, they migrate to their homes and fuck one another, passing diseases and using abortion as birth control - and those are the "lucky" ones. others jack off in bedrooms to youporn and ex-lovers with their right hands and battery operated devices.

then they wake up and do it all again and sadly, i'm one of them.

if you're going
to burn books
might as well
toss the ones
containing

statutes
codes
and laws

into a bonfire
in the middle
of town square

and let the
animals of this
world find out
who they really are

that'll be something
worth reading about.

he wants something serious:
dinner dates on friday nights
hikes every sunday morning
an espresso machine
meet the family
joint bank account
board games with friends

but

she wants something catastrophic:
whiskey kisses
hair pulling in bathroom stalls
scratches down her back
lipstick stains
make-up sex
cigarette drags at the edge of the bed

regardless, they keep trying
because she's everything he used to be
and he's everything she wants to become.

i hadn't updated my phone
so i didn't have
all the new emojis she did

and i didn't like
her instagram photos
as much as she wanted

so we broke up
and i wish her the best

with her new
emoji-using-instagram-liking
mother fucker

the brand spankin' new
operating system
she just had to download

sweet girl, just not for me.

those of us
who sit on our couch
and go 12 rounds
against ourselves

it's time
to throw in the towel
remove the gloves
head to our own corner

and learn to love all the
bruises and blood spots
on our bodies
that make us human.

i waited for you
as dogs do
on the edge
of the couch
for the mailman

but all you came
back with was
bills and bad news

and a
handwritten letter
saying i should stop
chasing my tail.

bright lime green
warnings on windows
chicken scratch written

by certain authorities
who eat high caloric donuts
in the morning

you must move this car
from the shoulder
within 72 hours

or the
automobile grim reapers
will tow it away

you ran out of fuel
before your exit, then took
an uber to the gas station

to purchase
a spill-proof can
of freedom that isn't free
and a white paper funnel

to replace
burning methane
three bucks on the gallon

you must move this car
within 72 hours

you must abide by our rules
you must not abandon it.

sit down at a blank surface
with a box of crayons

and draw giant house cats
attacking pirate ships
on coffee tables

no matter how old you are.

this old man pulls up a bar stool next to me and complains about the new digital jukebox. he's got these pale blue eyes and the slender face of a greyhound that's run one too many races. i order a grapefruit vodka and respond with a complaint of my own pertaining to my broken heart and he says to me:

"the only thing worse than falling out of love is staying with someone you don't and having to talk yourself into loving them every single day."

i hit ctrl-f to find you
in the giant document database
of this chaotic world

but the optical character recognition
program i used couldn't pick up
your handwritten text

so i'm left with unsearchable pages
that i'll read over and over again.

if 94 percent
of statistics
are made up

80 percent of me
wants to grab you
and kiss you

and say everything
is going to be
alright

the other 20
wants to give you

the finger.

my grandmother taught me
how to wash paint brushes
in her kitchen sink

how you brush them in a circle
on your palm until
the water is clear

"these are your tools – they are
just as important as your ideas"
she told me

"treat them kindly"

i suppose the same can be said
for all of us gentle humans

we must hold one another
with our callused hands
until the paint runs dry.

there is comfort in transition -
i find i’m at ease when
the seasons change

there’s liberation
on the open road
in an empty room
on a blank canvas
in a lonely heart

there’s hope in the sill
of a doorway
on the first of january

i wait for you there, patiently
like a marble stirring
yet still

eager to embrace
whatever transforms
so magically within you

this year.

i love the smell
of white-out
and gasoline

the former fixes
all of my mistakes

and the latter
(mixed w/ matches)

burns them all away.

we’re combining
1 part water
1 part sugar
and some honey
to make simple syrup
to mix with whiskey

she tells me about
this alternative stuff
called stevia
but i don’t have any
maybe next time

i rarely have everything
she wants
in my kitchen cabinets

as we light the flame
and heat it up
i’m reminded that
to survive
in a world like this

you need
1 part good
1 part evil
and a chip
on your shoulder

or else you get
swallowed up
like this alcohol

we’re about to
take down our throats.

we weren’t blinded by love
we were blinded by hope

hope that our love
would turn out different

than what decades worth
of data so clearly tells us.

my keys hang by the front door on a wall hook. my wallet sits on my dresser next to the same cologne i've worn for years. my watches are in an empty cigar box on my nightstand. my shirts are organized by purpose: work and leisure. the products under my kitchen counter look like they were merchandised by a supermarket clerk. my shoes are in a line on the rack in my closet, books alphabetized by author and my beers sit on the top shelf of my fridge standing shoulder to shoulder, ready for war. all of this fits perfectly in my studio apartment. she sends me a text on my way over to her house.

"i must warn you my room is a mess - everything is out of place."

i reply: "my stuff needs a home. your world can be total chaos and i won't mind being in it with you."

green protected arrows
create a false sense
of security

like promises whispered
from whiskey tongues
on a walk home
from the bar

the brilliant moon
stares down at us
and smirks

and she says
let's hit the gas
when we get home

baby, even
if it's only for tonight.

if we never truly know anyone
if we all live in tiny rooms
in our own heads

then love is two adjoined suites
where the door swings open
like a saloon from

time to time.

it's that time of night –

the drive-thru lines
are filled with humans
eager for their dollar menu fix

there are husbands
cheating on wives
and vice versa

there are politicians
getting naked dances

and a neurosurgeon in los angeles
snorting cocaine before his shift

but somehow
i can't find any of this behavior
listed on anyone's linkedin pages.

this tough guy pulls up next to me
at a stoplight in a leased mercedes

and “mean mugs” while blowing smoke
from his vape pen through the sunroof

i remember when i was a tough guy
and not a poet during a time in my life

it just meant keeping all the pain inside
because you’re too damn cool

to face whatever eats you up at night
so you try to devour other people all day.

i drive by a yellow house with a cherry door and a white picket fence. there is a fluorescent 'slow down' sign sitting on the curb, yelling at me to watch out for the children playing in the street. kids on bikes ride up and down the driveway and a lemonade stand sits unoccupied on the sidewalk, for business is slow. the grass is green of perfect length and spring is brewing in the soil, i can smell it. a flag hangs over the front window waving the red, white and blue. there's a lone leaf on the lawn and a picket is just out of place.

he sits on the toilet seat fully dressed with the shower running and a towel beneath the door. the fan is on, sucking up the smoke from the joint he rolled on the sink. in the living room you hear obama on the television: "on this day we gather because we have chosen hope over fear."

she stands at the kitchen counter tapping her wedding ring against a glass of chardonnay. it's half empty. a foreclosure document rests itself between a grocery list and other things she's yet to do. she stares out the window at the lemonade stand, knowing her daughter won't collect enough nickels.

dig your french
manicured nails
into my skull and

turn me into the
handsome robot
you so badly

want to control.

i’ve been around the world
i’ve walked the great wall
and marveled at big ben

without a plane ticket
or staying in hostels
or losing any luggage

instead, from the comfort of my ikea desk
with clicks of a mouse on google maps
i’ve traced her silhouette

on the back of my atlas
and traveled to the depths
of her wanderlust heart and back

with a first class ticket
staying in her bed
losing all of my luggage

but the distance ripped us apart
so i sit here alone at a laptop

viewing photos of beaches i’ll never visit
with pretty girls in bikinis i’ll never meet.

we both had a foot
out the door while
we tried to salvage
what was left but

that makes two feet
and two feet

is all you need
to walk away.

you told me not be a thief
as we stood within
a matchbook of aspen trees

you said “you took their
oxygen, now give it back”

you broke down the
chemistry of carbon dioxide
molecules in our breath

you took a swiss army knife
and carved our names
into a log – it was dead
so you could do that

you knew it wouldn’t decay
by winter’s end and
somehow

you knew we’d be back
again.

as i get older
my hangovers last longer
my muscles tire faster
my mind gets wiser

heartbreak doesn't feel like
heartbreak anymore

and the only things
i want to do

are the things that remind me
what it's like to be a kid
once again.

we swiped each other right on tinder
and she came out for the pride parade
for our first date

following the supreme court ruling
that declared same-sex marriage legal
in all fifty states, finally

and we did cocaine off my kitchen counter
and took bart to san francisco
and ended up in a sweaty gay bar

in the castro district where a man
was wearing nipple clamps
while dancing on a box

and then we met two gay brothers
on our way to dinner
and ate with them under the bay bridge

and then we took an uber home
and she did naked yoga in my living room
while an xx record spun

and then all morning i thought about why
it took humans that fucking long
in a democratic society

to be able to do what the fuck they want
when it doesn't harm anyone.

maybe we don't crave
everlasting love

maybe it's the falling
in and out we enjoy.

if you shed your body parts
to survive – i want them

i'll gather them like dead leaves
that trees discard so easily
during abscission

to withstand the freezing
temperatures of winter

that bite my lips
and sting my breath
and make me feel alive again.

she tells me
it's never too early
for whiskey –

"it's five o'clock
somewhere"

and
somewhere
somewhere
somewhere

someone is drinking
someone is fucking
someone is playing
with themselves

someone is praying
someone is sleeping
someone is dying
someone is being

born
into this ugly
precious world
we call home

it's five o'clock
somewhere

cheers.

let's take our judgmental eyes
and poke them out with
our middle fingers

make the criticisms
bleed down our tender faces
and let us see the world blind.

my flint-like fingers
spark as i strike
the surface of your
sterilized skin like
a bunsen burner and
hypothesize how your
inner blue flame
will make me feel
when the air in the
room fills with
moans and methane as
we naturally combust
into phosphorescent
ashes absorbed by
broiling bedsheets.

summer is gone and i've felt alone for weeks now. i haven't made your side of the bed for a month or had to separate your laundry into lights and darks. i'm turning on old sitcoms just to hear the laugh track in the background and facetiming friends who are far too busy to answer.

i end up playing solitaire against myself in an empty park trying to put two and two back together to figure out what the hell went wrong and where i can move my next card to the foundation in an attempt to change the outcome of this stupid little game.

she goes on for an hour
about capitalism
and working in cubicles
like a bunch of sheep

and how donald trump
is an idiot for the things
he says on television

and she ends this
entire rant by telling me
the worst thing ever is

fucking someone
with your socks still on.

i put a cardboard coaster
on my drink to reserve
my seat and you left

bite marks on my neck
scratches down my back
and scars on my heart

to notify my future lovers
this is your spot at the bar.

we twist through one q-tip a day, wipe through a roll of toilet paper every couple weeks, brush through a bottle of toothpaste on the monthly, fuck through a box of condoms twice a year (if you're lucky) and it takes over four hundred thousand gallons of water to bathe away a lifetime worth of sins.

then the earth swallows us up six feet under and all we leave behind are fingerprints on steamy shower walls as our naked children live on to do the same damn thing.

enjoy.

she’s crazy -
she’s got all these
bottles of wine she wants
to make wind chimes with

she’s got this purple mouth
and she wants to kiss me with it

and i tell her
“i’m glad you’re buzzed
because it takes a couple
glasses down the chute to
make you wanna kiss this beast”

she’s crazy and i’m crazy
and you’re crazy and
we all love it.

i've heard if you
start small and go big
in increments

you'll be able
to safely ingest
large amounts of poison

this could explain
how a lot of humans
are still with someone

they shouldn't be with.

i go through my receipts
and ticket stubs
jammed in the fold
of my wallet

searching for the note
you wrote me last week
when i was in a mood but

i can't find it
yet i know it's around

you're always around
even when i don't know
exactly where

and i like that.

my alarm goes off at 6:15 a.m. every morning, monday through friday. i hit the snooze button exactly three times. i park in spot 1106 and see the same seagulls circling over the parking lot at bayfair station as i transfer trains. i see the same man playing his acoustic guitar on 12th street, just a different song. he cycles through about five during the week as humans drop dollar bills into his empty case. i put two little containers of cream into my coffee, i use the same passwords for all of my accounts online, i greet each of my co-workers in a similar fashion and i take lunch at 12 p.m. every single afternoon. so, out of spite, i render enough courage and order the daily special at the corner cafe without even looking at the fucking menu.

we worry about
our confidential data
being leaked to the public

our medical records
our nudies
our credit card numbers

even though
our banks are backed
by the federal government

and we shouldn't be
so ashamed of our bodies
anyways

still, we worry
because nothing seems
entirely safe in the cloud

i remember reading
about an author or a poet
(i forget who it was)

who lost a briefcase
full of writing at some
train station in europe

and i remember wishing
there were firewalls
or auto computer locks
or some kind of way to track
your iphone back then

what a damn shame.

a red octagon
orange in the sun
demands me

to pause
for a moment
white letters control

my movements
but i just give it
a california stop

and roll on through...

most of the time when i visit yahoo it doesn't give me the answers i'm looking for so i have to go down the rabbit hole to google then reddit to quora then ask.com and if i still can't find whatever it is that will temporarily ease my anxious mind i'll post my sacred question on a message board in a dark alley on the internet but to be honest within an hour i typically forget why the hell it was important.

do you think
there's a soulmate
for everyone on earth?

i look at her
this gorgeous woman
knowing i won't be able
to give her what she needs
but goddamn i wish i could

and i respond:
i don't believe in fate –
i believe you can make
it work with many
different people
but some are
better for
you

than others.

she’s at the edge of my bed
after a one-night stand
buckling her shoes

i’m lying here
hungover as shit
and somewhat satisfied

wondering when these women
will see me less like a poem
and more like a novel.

the love you
give away
overnight

usually has an
early check-
out time.

as we decide what we want to drink she tells me her prince charming pets tigers. i haven't seen her in a while and she orders extra olives and twirls her straw as she explains exactly what she's looking for in a man: paul rudd's sense of humor, gosling's demeanor, gyllenhaal's smile, light eyes, dark hair, looks sharp in a suit but can throw on a flannel and grow a beard, steady income (or enough to buy her a nice purse every now and then and take her to the sushi place on the corner that has five stars on yelp), good credit, progressive but old-fashioned enough to open the door, and a man that has traveled the world and will take her with him when he embarks on another one of his adventures. that's the most important, she says, someone she can travel with. she pulls out her phone and shows me an example of said prince charming - a guy on match.com whom she's yet to message. he's tan and muscular and he's petting a goddamn tiger. i want a picture with a tiger, i think to myself. we chat a little more and say our goodbyes, until next time.

i get home, throw a record on, grab a magazine and take a shit – all the while wondering how the hell i'll ever meet up to these lofty expectations humans seem to have these days.

i remember as a child
learning to hand scissors

and how you keep
the blades in your palm
letting the recipient
grab the handles

and i think that's how
i'll give my heart
from now on

cautiously...
with the sharp parts
still in my chest

and the soft grips
extended outward

to avoid any accidents.

hummingbirds
flap their wings
at high frequencies

slow motion raindrops
fall against the window
outside

a load of laundry
goes through a cycle
of depression

classical music spins
on a phonograph
and tired neighbors

never look alive
the sun is hiding
behind black clouds

but don't you worry
it will return for you
tomorrow

or the next day -
i promise, it will return.

this “bum” sits on a bus stop bench near lake merritt drinking from a paper bag hopped up on mickey’s and tobacco watching the cars drive by and the lights change from green to yellow to red while people look at him and shake their heads yet he grins because...

he is content with having nothing and having nothing but content.

instead of synthetic love
drinks and boring table tops
alcohol and feel good drugs
checking our pulses for life

let's make this organic love
on top of mountain-tops
hiking trails side by side

sharing fresh oxygen and
checking our sun-kissed bodies
for ticks in the shower afterwards.

i'll take my typewriter to
some motel room in a town
somewhere i haven't been

where a neon sign flickers
in and out like certain parts
of my basic cable life

and pink plastic flamingos
read magazines in the dark
by the empty pool outside

i'll check in and cannonball
into the tiny bottles of alcohol
in the mini fridge

and then sit there naked
at a dusty desk
and write a little something

that hopefully fills up
your hollow soul.

you'll travel this world
alone
and there will be people

you learn to trust
and there will be people
you learn to leave

but there's always
sweet, sweet jazz

and handsome men
singing the blues
just for you.

somewhere
a man is fucking
an electric sex doll
instead of his wife

some new software
is writing poetry

a disc jockey
is pressing buttons
to make music

a program
is doing your job

a machine
is painting a mural

an algorithm
is feeding content
to the masses

a new cardiac device
that keeps a heart
beating forever

has been proven
to work on a rabbit

and now
you can download
a phone application
that shops for you

movies have told us
that robots could
take over the world

but we might just
become them.

i gave her the rough draft
of my book of poems
and she read it on
a 45 minute
train ride

from fremont to san francisco
and this is when i realized
the typical human life
can take decades to
write but

less than an hour to read.

it was raining last weekend
i was walking into lucky
to purchase a $6.99
pre-cooked rotisserie chicken

on discount because
it had been sitting out all day
and i realized

(or finally admitted to myself)
that the one thing that's kept me
from more love in my life

is my ego

that chicken didn't taste so good.

my late best friend
used to always tell me
that people never do grow up

the best relationships
consist of two adults playing tag
on an elementary school playground

last week i sat at a conference room table
with very smart minds in silicon valley
and noticed them twirl their pens
nervous to show and tell

wise beyond his years, he was
(my late best friend)
an old soul

we all expend so much energy
image crafting this pretty little
professional facade for the world

when all we want to do
is paint with our fingers
and play with our food

let us all remember to embrace
each and every day
with the innocence of our youth.

she looked the devil
straight in the eyes
and told him

i don't want this halo
you're handing me if
you're just going to

hold it over my head.

this swedish girl i meet at starbucks pulls the get up for “something” and walk back trick to grab my attention without making it too obvious. it works and we make eye contact and she says “hi” – saying it loud enough to puncture the headphones i have in. she’s reading a book titled “boundaries” and i ask her why and she explains that she has a hard time saying “no” to people. i’m tempted to ask her to buy me a venti iced coffee with room for cream and maybe even one of those expensive stainless steel travel mugs but i refrain and ask for her phone number instead.

“maybe i should test this book out right now,” she says.

staring at rubber bar mats
i search for you

in bottles full of backwash
and glass cups
with leftover foam
from golden beers

are you there?

or does this music
make me feel like you are.

how much alcohol
needs to be
running

through your veins
for you to tell me...

does this need to be
a 5k or a goddamn
marathon of
top-shelf
liquor

for you to tell me
that you love
me

only me

and for you to
take it all back

in the morning.

you get older and start expecting less from people. she gave her best friend's boyfriend a handjob in the bathroom at the same party. he's back in rehab for the third time – same shit, different drug. the family on the corner with the white picket fence are swingers every first friday of the month. the well-dressed man with two free hands let the door slam in my face at starbucks this morning. the girl i met on eharmony was absolutely horrible in bed. at the end of the day i'm a happy man if the newspaper makes it on my porch before breakfast and my water glass gets filled twice by the waitress at dinner.

don’t tell me to pour my heart
into an empty scotch glass

if you aren’t going to
kick your shoes off

and enjoy it
with me.

i’m the color
of the nail polish palette
she can’t settle on

her bare feet
dipped in a sorbet
of bubbles, hair up
headphones in and

i’m a color,
gender neutral,
somewhat strong
and very vulnerable

i’m a color
she just can’t settle on

but her toes look good.

i've fallen in love less than a handful of times,
each one a unique variation of the word

young and innocent
unhealthy and possessive
deep and passionate
friendly and platonic

so when she asked who i fell for first
i had to respond that they all felt brand new

like an odyssey into their separate souls
with different pieces of my heart
with different parts of my mind

and i'm sure as i grow old i'll fall again
for different women
for the first time.

people have said
(friends and family)
“you’re too deep”

and for a while
i saw it as a flaw
so i tried to

hide it
change it
self-medicate it

nothing worked
nothing at all
so i’m still my
“too deep self”

but embracing it
has been
much more fun.

i remember her complaining
about the wind at the beach
that day

as we collected skeletons
in our socks
made of calcium carbonate

that tiny critters leave behind
when they pass away

“oysters were once
food for the poor”
she mentioned

“now they’re treated poorly by
the rich who don’t appreciate
them quite like they should”

i said something stupid
about how they are
also aphrodisiacs
(the oysters,
not the rich)

and she laughed
and she turned me on
when she said things like that

about how the upper class
tends to ruin everything.

go have one more dance
with the sun, before it sets

right there
on the horizon line

have one more dance alone
but when the darkness falls
on your shoulders

and the street lamps turn on
i hope you come home.

they lie in bed at opposite ends
struggling to find the amper-
sand between their names

left with (parenthetical pillows)
dividing them like back\slashes
and blank words only a spacebar

could   create.

she tells me it's been months without human contact. without the warmth of another human soul. without flipping over the pillow because it's too fucking cold. and i've been there before – when you drive through drive-thrus and order only a diet coke to brush hands with a stranger while they give you change.

and at this time you don't mind crowded elevators even though they make you claustrophobic because the shoulder of the man next to you feels nice. you can hear his music in his headphones, you can feel his heartbeat in your bones, you can see his pain on his fingertips. you want to ask him where he keeps the rest of it.

you get so wrapped up in things: your life, responsibilities, the colors of your socks. the voices in your head that disguise themselves as thoughts. days go by, weeks, and then years and you forget how you just want to be held like your mother held you when your father was at work. like the person you once loved, you thought you'd always love, like they held you.

and now, each day, you fall in love over and over again, from a safe distance, with people you won't see tomorrow, with people who won't remember you tomorrow. but maybe that's how it's supposed to be.

you'll reflect
about ex-lovers
and wonder

how they forgot
so soon and
you remember
so violently.

sometimes i hear your voice
in these songs by the ataris,
brand new, and taking
back sunday and
sometimes

i remember all the
high school parties
drinking plastic bottle vodka

we purchased with fake
identification and
sometimes

i drive these streets and
pop in old compact discs
that seem to have captured
more than i burned in them

and sometimes i get high
on my younger years
and remember

nostalgia is a helluva drug
best served in moderation.

in high school i tried
too hard to be cool

in college i thought
i was too cool

now i know
i'm not that cool

and i think that's
pretty fuckin' cool.

my mom always said
you don't say i love you
for at least six months

and until you've known them
for all four seasons
you don't give them your trust

so take it easy on the shots
and savor some bourbon
with ice in a glass

in lieu of serving up your heart
with cinnamon, no back.

i've realized the meaning of life
only a handful of times –

lying on the living room floor
of my apartment in san diego

one time driving down
foothill road back home

and another walking market street
on a blurry city night
the concrete buildings seemed
to have all the answers

sketched into them and the lights
provided a moment of
absolute truth

a moment of absolute certainty

but in these moments
i've never had a pen
to write any of it down.

there is nothing
complicated
about humans

besides the fact
that humans like
to complicate

everything.

she comments on your furniture. the secondhand stuff you picked up from the hospital on the corner. ad on craigslist read: "old couch and some chairs from the waiting room, might need a little tlc." it's been a while since you've seen her. she says you need more art on your walls. girls have a way of dressing up your apartment with their eyes. dressing you up with their eyes. you try to explain you haven't had the chance to grab your paintings from storage where they reside in bubble wrap, but her face says she doesn't want any explanations. she's been here five minutes and she's already giving you a helluva time. you take a drag from your glass as the ice clinks against the sides.

"your apartment is so...cold."

you offer her some whiskey to warm things up, but she denies.

"you know what will happen if i do that."

the tapping starts – her nails on the back of her iphone. you sense it's different this time around, like this isn't the same as picking up a bike. you get up to feed your fish on the kitchen counter. it swims around the bowl, waiting for the food to sink to the bottom. the ice jiggles in your glass, her tapping moves from her phone to the armrest on your hospital chair and you begin to doubt that time heals everything – something you've accepted as absolute fact. you feel like you're to blame. like you're the captain of this miniature shipwreck, rummaging through wooden casks at the bottom of the boat for final sips. she ends up leaving, giving you a half-hug on the doorstep – one of those hugs where she barely wraps one arm around your side and looks down the sidewalk as she pulls away. you head back inside and remember someone telling you once that all time does is narrow the scope.

as a writer
i sometimes feel
like the older skipper
spitting sunflower seeds

on the dugout floor
teaching these kids how
to play but watching them

run the bases.

okay, i'll write about you
one more time, about
your delicate yellow dress

that your mom bought you
that you wore to the party
that i threw
that hot summer night

it came off towards the end
in my bedroom and
we made love

even though they say
you can't make love
when it's only
the first time

well, they don't know
what the hell they're
talking about.

i remember an age
building treehouses,
playing football in the street
and chasing down
the ice cream man

i remember an age
with scavenger hunts,
knocking on neighbors' doors
for a paperclip or an apple
or whatever we made up
to track down

and i remember an age
using nickels in the arcade
at the bowling alley
when americans weren't afraid
to actually cultivate
human relationships

we weren't all fucking paranoid
and divided
and self-medicated
and distant

then technology was created
to bring us all together
but what it really does
is keep us in our houses

i remember an age
when i felt free
and it wasn't all so complicated.

i can no longer
be your source

for instant
gratification.

the world is hungover
today,
for most
kissed the bottle

some kissed a lover
some kissed a stranger
some even had the courage
to kiss nothing at all

but here we are –
all of us
deciding if we want to
crack open another beer,
to keep our drunk going
from last year

or grab opposite ends
of that beautiful
porcelain toilet bowl,
throw it all up

and move on.

we were drunk
werewolves
that night

throwing bottles
at the moon
and howling

about the fact
that life seems
to shapeshift

before we've
had the chance
to truly enjoy it.

some think graffiti
is a pup pissing
on a fire hydrant

pour souls
claiming their territory
claiming their corner

sayin' don't come
around here no more –

there will be violence
in this bathroom
there will be violence
in this stall

there will be sex
there will be drugs
there will be love
in a lap dance

take it or leave it
but we're writing
our names
on your skin
with a needle

and you won't
have any regrets.

i’ve wandered, exhaustingly
within the walls of my mind

it’s now time for me
to wander with my feet

in search for whatever i find.

in fifth grade i missed the bus
the last day of elementary school

normally i would call mom
but i felt like a big boy
in the moment

so i walked home
damn near twelve blocks
through the streets of san jose

even stopped at mcdonald's
for a large strawberry milkshake
with leftover lunch money

i didn't tell mom about it
until i was around eighteen
and she just shook her head
and laughed
and knew she wasn't ready
for the truth back then

and sometimes humans
just aren't ready for the truth at all
parents, lovers, enemies, friends

they aren't ready
for your independence
for certain decisions that you'll make
for certain desires that sit in your heart

like heavy stones and this is when
you just walk home and this is when
you just walk to wherever home is.

you don't have to wear black
to a funeral, my mom said
my little sister in an obsidian dress

i threw a blue shirt on
to go witness death, yet again
people die in many ways

hemingway used a shotgun
plath stuck her head in a stove
for bukowski it was leukemia
and some say nietzsche had syphilis

yesterday we paid our respects
to my grandmother's best friend
who passed away from old age
the best way to go, if there is a best

people die in many ways
people live in many ways too

we watched a video of her dancing
filmed a week before her death
she had so much life in her still

and i thought that's how i want to live.

go be yourself
sing the blues
dance to jazz

go find darkness
chase it - if you’re
scared of the sun

go get kicked out
of every bar
even if there is
only one in town

today is yours
tomorrow is yours
just don’t be
someone else...

i'm pissing in this urinal
in some diner off the 101
and take it easy
by the eagles comes on

"don't let the sound
of your own wheels
drive you crazy"

i realize i've been spendin'
a lot of time alone lately

i eat alone
i drink alone
i fuck myself a lot

i sit up and turn around
to this mirror of graffiti
staring back at me

someone drew a smiley face
in bright red sharpie
and glenn frey's singin'

"lighten up while you still can."

take it easy...

Made in the USA
Middletown, DE
14 February 2018